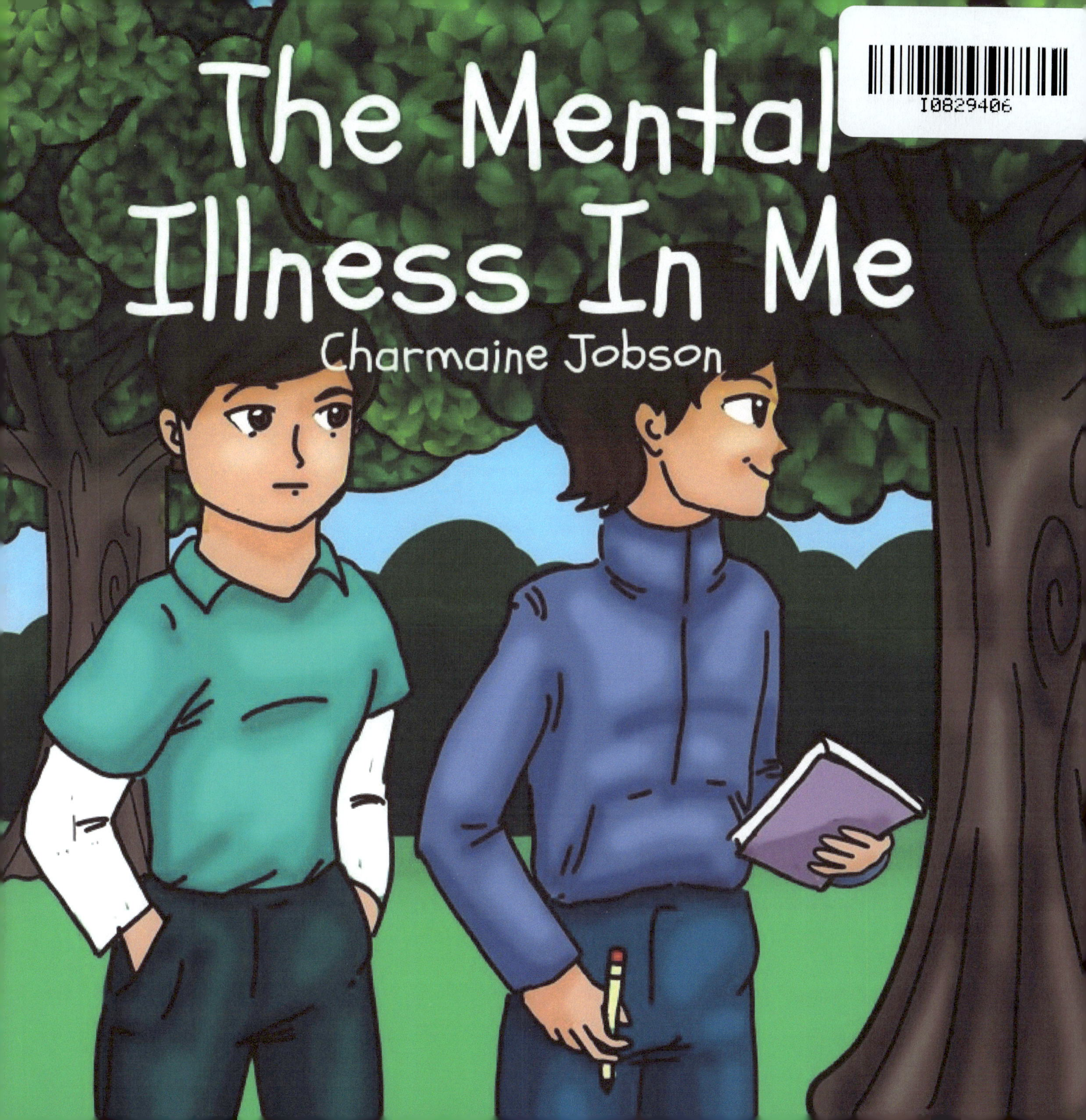

The Mental Illness In Me
Charmaine Jobson
I0829406

The Mental Illness In Me
"The Issue of Life Series"

Copyright © 2018

Published 2018 by Charmaine Jobson

Illustrations by: J. Gutierrez

Cover designed by: RebecaCovers
Book layout by: www.diverseskillscenter.com

Printed in the United States of America
ISBN-13: **978-1986760133**

ISBN-10: 1986760138

For Those
with Mental Illness

With Love,
C.J.

"Johnny, why are you talking to yourself?" asked Tristin. "I am talking to my imaginary friends," said Johnny.

"Do they answer you?" asked Tristin with a puzzled look on his face.

"Does your friends answer you?" asked Johnny with a smug smile.

Johnny always has his notebook and pencil with him. He just sits by himself and write all day. Today, he wrote a poem and wanted Tristin to hear it.

He took out his notebook and started to read, as a look of sadness came over him.

POEM

"So much mental illness in
the world today,
Many have nowhere to stay.

They sleep under bridges and
live on the streets,
Smiling at everyone they
meet."

"Some have a faraway look in
their eyes,
Others just stand and stare
at passersby."

"Mothers and fathers are confounded,
Brothers and sisters are astounded.
How could this be happening to us they cry,
No answers to be gotten, just lies, lies, lies."

"Shame begins to slowly
creep in,
Mental illness they say is
caused by sin.

Before you know it, the
blame game starts,
Which tears many families
apart.

Disassociate yourself,
relatives shout!
But the truth has a way of
leaking out."

"Trying to get help is an
arduous task,
It's like everyone is wearing
a blank mask."

Some people say put them
out on the street,
The police comes along and
say, "Get in the back seat!"

Off they go to the County jail
or Behavioral Center,
Medication make some take
a turn for the better."

"For others, Bus Stop is
their favorite place,
The seat allows them a
part-time space."

And for a few, it's a bench
in the Park,
Where several unknown
humans visit after dark."

"Then the cycle starts all
over again,
Another life gone down the
drain.

No one cares enough to break the chain,
Of injustice towards the mentally insane."
BEHAVIORAL CENTER

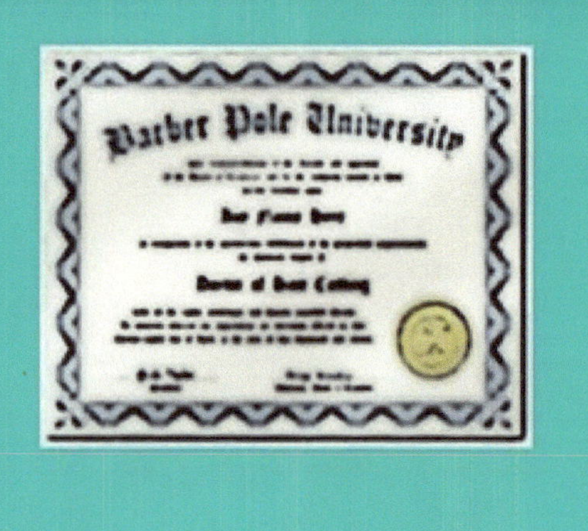
Barber Pole University
Doctor of Hair Cutting

Para Nobel State University
Doctor of Pare Ba

UNIVERSIDAD DE SANTANDER

"Do your part, get involved today,
Help stop the cycle of mental illness replay.

Become an advocate for a brother or sister,
And reach out to that crying father or mother."

"Tristin, do you like it?"
asked Johnny, waiting with
anticipation for his friend's
reply.

Tristin was too choked up to
speak. He looked at Johnny,
smiled and nodded with tears
in his eyes. "Johnny is this
poem about you?

"Not about me, but it
happened to a few people I
know," said Johnny with a
wink.

"Johnny, please keep taking your medication and whenever you need to talk, I will always be here for you," said Tristin.

Tristin couldn't fully understand what was going on in Johnny's head and what causes him to react the way he does, but one thing he knew for sure, is that Johnny's mental illness would not stop them from being best friends.

The End

You can contact us for the "Issues of Life" series of books, speaking engagements, or bulk purchases for school libraries and book stores.

Chatty Mc, Inc.
P.O. Box
678733
Orlando, FL 32867

www.chattymc.com

Other products from
The Issues of Life Series

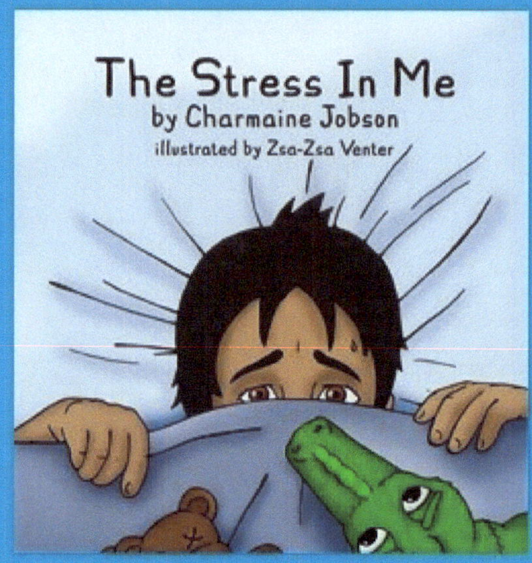

Children are a product of their parents and environment. Adults may not be aware that they are teaching their child, life-long lessons by their own behavior. Parents can ensure positive actions by creating a safe, peaceful, loving, nurturing environment. Maximize your time with your children by interacting with them and exercising parental control.

Read about Jordan's emotionally stressful day at school and how his stress was eliminated. The "ISSUES OF LIFE" series is designed to help parents and educators teach children how to prevent lifelong consequences.

You can find this book on Amazon -http://amzn.to/2ug3o1Y